THESE **SUPER**BRIGHT IDEAS BELONG TO _____

_____

SPARK OF GENIUS

SPARK OF GENIUS

SPARK OF GENIUS

SPARK OF GENIUS

SPARK OF GENIUS

SPARK OF GENIUS

SPARK OF GENIUS

SPARK OF GENIUS

SPARK OF GENIUS

SPARK OF GENIUS

SPARK OF GENIUS

SPARK OF GENIUS

SPARK OF GENIUS

SPARK OF GENIUS

SPARK OF GENIUS

SPARK OF GENIUS

FRUITFUL OUTCOMES

FRUITFUL OUTCOMES

FRUITFUL OUTCOMES

FRUITFUL OUTCOMES

FRUITFUL OUTCOMES

FRUITFUL OUTCOMES

FRUITFUL OUTCOMES

FRUITFUL OUTCOMES

FRUITFUL OUTCOMES

FRUITFUL OUTCOMES

COTTON CANDY DREAMS

COTTON CANDY DREAMS

COTTON CANDY DREAMS

COTTON CANDY DREAMS

COTTON CANDY DREAMS

COTTON CANDY DREAMS

COTTON CANDY DREAMS

COTTON CANDY DREAMS

COTTON CANDY DREAMS

COTTON CANDY DREAMS

COTTON CANDY DREAMS

COTTON CANDY DREAMS

COTTON CANDY DREAMS

COTTON CANDY DREAMS

ULTRAVIOLET VISIONS

ULTRAVIOLET VISIONS

ULTRAVIOLET VISIONS

ULTRAVIOLET VISIONS

ULTRAVIOLET VISIONS

ULTRAVIOLET VISIONS

ULTRAVIOLET VISIONS

LIMELIGHT ASPIRATIONS

LIMELIGHT ASPIRATIONS

LIMELIGHT ASPIRATIONS

LIMELIGHT ASPIRATIONS

LIGHTNING STRIKES

LIGHTNING STRIKES

LIGHTNING STRIKES

LIGHTNING STRIKES

LIGHTNING STRIKES

LIGHTNING STRIKES

LIGHTNING STRIKES

LIGHTNING STRIKES

LIGHTNING STRIKES

LIGHTNING STRIKES

LIGHTNING STRIKES

LIGHTNING STRIKES

LIGHTNING STRIKES

LIGHTNING STRIKES

LIGHTNING STRIKES

LIGHTNING STRIKES

LIGHTNING STRIKES

LIGHTNING STRIKES

LIGHTNING STRIKES

LIGHTNING STRIKES

LIGHTNING STRIKES

LIGHTNING STRIKES

LIGHTNING STRIKES

LIGHTNING STRIKES